—away!

By Janine Amos and Annabel Spenceley

Consultant Rachael Underwood

CHERRYTREE BOOKS

A Cherrytree Book

Designed and produced
by A S Publishing

Copyright this edition © Evans Brothers Ltd 2003
by Cherrytree Press Ltd
327 High St
Slough
Berkshire
SL1 1TX

First published in 1999

First published in paperback 2003

British Library Cataloguing in Publication Data

Amos, Janine
  Go away!. – (Good friends)
  1.Friendship – Pictorial works – Juvenile literature
  I. Title II.Annabel Spenceley
  302.3'4

ISBN 1 84234 153 7

Printed and bound in Malaysia

Grandma's story

Ben is watching a caterpillar.

Grandma is reading a story.

Ben looks up. He wants to join in.
Ben goes over to Grandma.

He crawls on to her lap.
He crawls all over Luke.

"Go away!" shouts Luke.

How do you think Ben feels?

"Luke, I think Ben wants to listen, too,"
says Grandma.

Ben nods his head.
"But I was here first," says Luke.

"You all want to sit on my lap," smiles Grandma.
"I wish I had a giant's lap!"

12

"What could we do?" asks Grandma.
What do you think they could do?

"I'll sit right next to you – and Ben can
sit on my lap!" says Patrick.

"Yes!" says Ben.

"Now we've got two laps to share!"
laughs Grandma.

The shop

Naisha has made a shop.
She puts out the apples, the eggs
and the bread.

Here comes Maggie.
"I'll be the shopkeeper!" she says.
"You can buy my things."

Maggie picks up some stones.
"This can be the money."

"Go away!" shouts Naisha.

Steve looks in. "Naisha, you sound upset," he says.
"What's Maggie doing that you don't like?"

"She wants to be the shopkeeper – and
I'm the shopkeeper!" says Naisha.

24

"But I want to sell things too!" says Maggie.
"Mmm," says Steve.
"So you both want to be shopkeepers?"

"Yes," agrees Maggie.
Naisha nods.

"I know!" says Naisha.
"We could have two shopkeepers!"

"But who will be the customer?"
wonders Maggie.

Maggie looks at Naisha.
Naisha looks at Maggie.

They both look at Steve.

"Steve can!" they shout together.

"Go away!" lets someone know that you don't like what they're doing. But they may feel upset by the words.

Instead, think about what you would like. Tell the other person. If you both want different things, perhaps you can solve the problem by talking about it.